HOUSE
(BLOWN APART)

A Book of Poems

Other books of poetry
by David Shapiro

HOUSE
(BLOWN APART)

A Book of Poems

DAVID SHAPIRO

THE OVERLOOK PRESS
Woodstock, New York

Some of these poems have appeared in the following publications: *The American Poetry Review, The Paris Review, Scripsi, Express, Boulevard, Notus, New Observations, Normal, Little Magazine, Journal, Parkett, Precis* 6, and *Architectures.*

First published in 1988 by
The Overlook Press
Lewis Hollow Road
Woodstock, New York 12498

Copyright © 1988 by David Shapiro
Designed by Abigail Sturges

Library of Congress Cataloging-in-Publication Data

Shapiro, David, 1947 –
House (blown apart).

I. Title.
PS3569.H34H6   1988   811'.54   87-28329

ISBN: 0-87951-310-1 (cloth)
ISBN: 0-87951-331-4 (paper)

To my son

CONTENTS

HOUSE (BLOWN APART)

for John Hejduk

HOUSE (BLOWN APART)

I can see the traces of old work
Embedded in this page, like your bed
Within a bed. My old desire to live!
My new desire to understand material, raw
Material as if you were a house without windows
A red stain. Gold becomes cardboard.
The earth grows rare and cheap as a street.
Higher up a bird of prey affectionate in bright gray
     travels without purpose.
I beg you to speak with a recognizable accent
As the roof bashed in for acoustics
Already moans. What is not a model
Is blown to bits in this mature breeze.
If students visit for signs
Or signatures we would discuss traces.
     We would examine each other for doubts.
Old work we might parody as an homage
Losing after all the very idea of parody.
Traces of this morning's work are embedded in this page.

LIMITS

My father had some curious things to say
About limits, in a dream:
I would not be a curator of the skin
Without knowing the inside of the body.
Think of a general practitioner in Omaha
Keeping up. Think of the optic nerve
Connected to everything, in a sense.
At seventy, one feels seeing and sees feeling.
Then doctor and body crack like a green sea bottle.

THE CUP IN ARCHITECTURE

There is the cup, and there is the broken cup,
And there is trouble in the broken cup.
Or is there trouble with the broken cup?
Is there a collaborative plot, and is there glue?
They have begun repair too soon,
Like details of an eyelid in father's clay,
    Details prepared for a death mask of a city.

It is the cup of a psychotic doctor
On a "talk show" who "acts out"
And puts his feet in the lap of the host
And knocks over the cup without apology.
It is the cup as apology, and the cup without doubts.
It criticizes your work and its simplicity
Because it is evident the cup is finite now
And you had arranged to forget its nomad margins.

In the middle of the country lies a broken university
And there they think of the cup
And its analogies. As the cup to the difficult test
So our broken music and what we think and may
Not think. I ask you to paint the cup
A grave, a cartoon character, and the night sky.
But you have the idea as friend
And certainty is lying there, like a broken cup.
And the lover says Break it, as you broke us.

One has drawn a lozenge in space, shattering
All pastels and later tilting in a more regular
Horizon. You note the archaic horizon
And accuse the present of a lying fold.
Secret waves are breaking: abundance, enigmagram.

I show you the book of Rome: a shriveled
Shell. Embarrassed by pictures,
Clutching at the models like ledges, I ask
Questions about tea: Would you choose
Of the cup, tea or expensive clothes—say
In prison? The laws are insults, insults prisons.
What are you thinking of that is not the broken cup?
We who consume the word, not the elixir.
There must be thirst for the broken cup.

The cup is buried alive, in sand.
The person knocked in the head with wine.
We know or might know now, says the dream,
That such a blow kills the person and keeps
The juices from flowing to the brain.
Nor will children repair it again, like a mother.

You have written in the shape of a house.
Your brother romps in mud outside.
Inside, the sadistic night-calls.
With death a normal life resumes.
The cup lies on the pavement, in stars and stone.

On the road home, you cure a lame old man and give
    him a house.

THE BLANK WALL

"The blank wall is on its way to becoming (sic)
The dominant feature of U.S. downtowns
These are not inadvertent blank walls. These
Walls were meant to be blank." It wasn't a letter,
It was your life; I delivered it in light rain
To the Architectural League. I am amazed at the
Blank wall, it is so expensive, as others
Are amazed that they have brought back the blank wall.
"Oh, the blank wall is so terrible." The grace notes
Strike against it. She is not feeling much,
The blank wall. With beaded bubbles winking on
The blank wall. This happened once to a colossal
Vault of sexual objects in indeterminate cast.
Careless curators, oxymoronically engaged.
The grave stone has a name, it says "Name."
Ah, Hamlet was fat and the jump into the grave
And the temper tantrum, for example,
Will not work. It does not dissolve
The blank or minister to nonangels in the mood
Of sulking brother. Dark, dark, dark, you may
All jump into the dark in a mania of lack
Of doubt. Dark, blank wall, we will stay beside you
And try to learn the lesson without the teacher.
There is nothing behind the blank wall, not even the
    broken cup.

TRACING OF AN EVENING

A man and a woman recite their dreams
In places of fear: a bell tower, behind the blinds, a bridge.
Snow falls on the phonograph
On architecture and poetry.

The prodigal has finished a visit.
The old man was watching from a book.
For so long the narcissus has rotted.
The floor is so far from the earth.

This is where nomads fall upwards
To say nothing in favor of physical pain.
One finds the ocean more transparent,
One finds the ocean more opaque.

A VISIT FROM THE PAST

On George Washington Bridge.
In negative rain and sleet.
The bridge is fine but not
Its present paltry state.

But one concentrates on a blur:
My book slightly ripped,
Yours not merely human.
All one sees is a photographer.

Mother is burning her father
In layers of newspaper.
In the street it softly falls;
It is a public funeral.

And the critic cries: It is gray!
Yes, but so is grass or your hat.
Like a photograph of hands or a stairway,
criticism could be like love, specific.

She crosses the street to say:
I will be afraid for both of us.
She gives you her laughter: a
rare colorful vase.

Maps of the present fall from me
with exits, entrances, names of the judges, the judged.
Unrecognized, I am so happy.
I shake hands with the past.

TRAUMEREI

One fine day,
open as cut lips,
more than alive—asleep and beaten powerless
you and I
like students evacuating
a burning high school
then lying flat like a drunken one next to the old boiler
in a T-shirt consumed by snow
when us the janitor awakens
we shall be
heated like dead languages after school
safe still, exempt on the illegal floor
in the high observatory
we will pardon the imbeciles
as clear, as intelligible
hardly have time for the brain that kills, bravo
then walking back to school, resolved
under the branches flinging marks
the snow is more than alive, it is asleep
in the little nut-brown street
infamous as sleet as the day repeats
Look at yourself! Look at yourself! That's why
        I'm driving you away
With my infra-red powerful ray
In the absence of a sphere of Lucky Socrates!
Lucky Socrates!
Almost too seriously, and frighteningly, oh sleep.

TAKING A FERRY

Flying onto a ship in heavy fog
Then you appear. Outside, a star.
Some do not look, in fear,
Because we are in outer space,
    a kind of college.

Try to make life something other
Then simply *not unbearable.*
Talk of a show of nomad architects.
Could it be one is trying to
    destroy architecture.

Then go off to build a commodity
And something falls on us like a trick.
Your shirt has been stamped with
    comic strips.
This scene "would be good with music."

You encircle me like a book
As I am reading: A movie of your mother
Nude from the waist up and singing
As a cardboard cutout. Only the voice is preserved.

It's a film of music and threats and mother's breast
Pressed against the glass of a screen.
School? Painting? Oh we are taking a bus
Death says it's ridiculous to give you more time to polish.

A WALL

I have the right not to represent it.

Though every brick is clear as a doubt
Clear as a tear and as a mistranslation
Through the window as through December fourth
The clarity of the facts like light snow
After bad dreams forgotten partly whole
And of the whole a part
One may forget so intently you might write

"I cannot now respond to this abstraction
Unshareable satire, courtly dream, and so forth
Sorry, not sorry" But try as I shall not to bump
Or bash it or lift a camera to a sill
To penetrate a copy or to think I have invented it

A banal impossibility as night is written
In pages splitting into analogies like walls
I see in this quiet sunlit stylization
Holding forth onto a garden enclosed and yet at times
Open in a melancholy necessary morning:

A wall I neither restored nor could destroy.

IN A BLIND GARDEN

The whale
is a room
A light blue room
a blind garden
The skulls make room too
And what is the whale
behind you
It's a complex note
When the whale strains
The little fish die
must die like a school
of lances trained on
our friend of two openings
a blowhole a slippery
prey pointed like a joint
in a design of teeth
Can you guess
which whale
Imagine you are a
whale: what a waste
of captured energy
Jonah sulking
like light in a pyramid

and the summer eats
through you like an
island or like
an island whale
with a huge watery tongue
pushing Jonah to that
elusive depth
where the jaw's

sounds pierce him
ear to ear: it is
fear, fear of the bottom
fear of the crashing filter
of these open mouths
skinning us, squeezing
us and gulping our happy eyes
Jonah stands naked in the
room with no solutions
throwing lots like a blanket

and the whale also drowns
like he/she slightly singing
The first part to break
is the hole tightly closed
Next the subject
Next the streamlined shape
As we are young
we have reached the zero surface
Mother's nipple our first meal
nurses for two years
the richest of all animals
Jonah, grow on this
rich milk
in the unique ribs
collapsing under pressure
like Nineveh of grime
The airplane learns
the song is almost continuous
and the prophet's perfume
is then engraved with a picture
The scratches are filled with soot

In a blind garden
think of the whale

as helping Jonah
a joke in poor taste
in relation to a lack
of consciousness of nonsense
Now think of Nineveh
of madness and associated cities
Dear whale of my youth
you are alive and I am swallowed
Now think of a rotting palm
of a rotting royal palm
under which you dream
of a curse like sperm or teeth
of a continuing city's fine song
that can never be heard
by idiotic ears

the prophet's a skeleton now
what about a coral skull
or a coral penis
or coral without the body
We must blind one another
like pollen in the bright
sun's dust Mercifully
mercy concludes the story
Your dreams are those
of a young architect
You don't want to be seen, but to inspect
the curious architecture
of the island bird's throat
as you grow aware of the
increasing dark green ground
of the truncated future

ARCHAIC TORSOS

after a dream

You must change your life fourteen times.
Change your way of living like writing.
You must change your method and your mind. You
Have to transform life fourteen times. Change life.
It has become necessary to change your life.
You need this change. We need to change your life.
And now you'd better change it: you, yourself.
It's up to you to exchange your life. Change, change!
Alter your life, patch and reshape your life.
"A change come o'er the spirit of your change."
You might shuffle the cards spin wheels change wheels.
You must convert resolve revolutionize your dissolves.
You might change life itself. And you might change.
You must change. You must not outlive your life.

IN MEMORY OF POETRY

In memory of a collection of sculpture, in memory of chains,
Margins, in memory of a concordance of flowers of good, in
    memory
Of the reader over the dice cup, in memory of late human
    shows and earlier
Like a gun in the bottle, in memory of the flowering lady and
    the palace plum, in memory of the masters eroding like
    summer haze,
In memory while the profile of liberty rusts, in memory of the
    green
Journals like a child at the center of the earth, in memory
Of memory not that drawings will stop falling with power
    upon robots
And empire and city, but that small grave steles fall apart,
In memory like ill-beloved winter words.

A PIN'S FEE, OR PAINTING WITH STAR

The frame of the world is suddenly rotated
and the change flows through you like a mosaic of diseases
you are sealed off in a room at the bottom, fixed with stars
your earth and your magnet and your little red life

like the desire to cast the image of a woman
on a wall distant as a lamp
a dead body traveling north like an empty house, burning
High above the acanthus
stands the Siren, mourning the outlines
of a spiral

The dead are exceptionally rapt
The hair falls, freely rendered
A work well delineated if cold
Artemis, headless

Recollection sustains a sound
like a music with thorns
You were always softer, always later
in the oblique
like the uncalled-for summer's end

It is as if a clamp had been placed
over the bridge
preventing your voice
not just a sourdine, but the variations of your voice
        your brisk commands

It is a very ancient instrument
the smothered harp

you and I could scarcely sustain
    that first attack
quickly to war but all love studies liberty
and we have hated to hate
like the blue lieutenants and pastel constraints
dwarf mirrors and mirrors for clothes and time poured
    on mirrors of flesh

There is only one secret: the old stylelessness
freedom to visit the fugitives
("You are not a stove. Well, do you mean to insinuate
a person might be a stove")
And in winter we put up storm windows and felt around the
    doors

If there is only one bed
no matter how thick
There is only one air
Two window sashes, one air,
two walls, two shirts, some hollow birds
Black wax: those birds look like houses made of hollow bricks

You already a half ghost
and anyone speaking to you or drawing you even half a ghost
and then you become a whole and drop out of the game
and anyone who is half a ghost and speaks to you
becomes whole and drops out of the game

I am drawing your outline now
by memory
a quiet game which is always a way
and I am trying to place the lakes, rivers
and life's dust within a few miles of where they belong

A BOOK OF GLASS

On the table, a book of glass.
In the book only a few pages with no words
But scratched in a diamond-point pencil to pieces in diagonal
Spirals, light triangles; and a French curve fractures lines to
    elisions.

The last pages are simplest. They can be read backwards and
    thoroughly.
Each page bends a bit like ludicrous plastic.
He who wrote it was very ambitious, fed up, and finished.
He had been teaching the insides and outsides of things

To children, teaching the art of Rembrandt to them.
His two wives were beautiful and Death begins
As a beggar beside them. What is an abstract *persona*?
A painter visits but he prefers to look at perfume in vials.

And I see a book in glass—the words go off
In wild loops without words. I should
Wake and render them! In bed, Mother says each child
Will receive the book of etchings, but the book will be
    incomplete, after all.

But I will make the book of glass.

THE LOST GOLF BALL

THE LOST GOLF BALL

Part of the universe is missing
Sings or says the newspaper, and I believe it.
Even most of it. As tape runs out of a typewriter. Big
    surprise:
And it won't do to go looking for holes
Or changes in the constitution of matter
Like a rare jewel in a crossword puzzle
Or yourself as an answer
Linking and locking up space
In the accidental field where you stumble
Like a star lost on a white ceiling
Parts of the universe are missing
The random minor stars you improvised
Litter the mind but might not go out
Damned to hell not what are you but
Where are you my poem
Nothing is left but the recantation
The repetition in a glut
Miraculous as evil
Joining the democracy of pain as if to improve it
A woman like Venice and like Venetian blinds
Opening and closing
Part of the universe is missing. Missing!

Is this our bedroom or a planetarium?

The title could be an inducement like a lost ball
though it never appears in the final painting
though anything might, a buried ship, the title is a nude
but the title is not a can opener or a handle for a pot
Sometimes what is lost does make an appearance however
taking a common revenge like a word

Losing the lost golf ball, find the lost golf ball
The title itself is a ceiling for
stars that shine at night, will not fade, and stick by themselves
like a slogan
"You have made my room a universe," as you said you would

A METAPHOR

My students had curiously little to say
About metaphor, in a dream:
The window-cleaners broke through the window.
As your mother pushed into the ragged house
In a fur several sizes too small for her body
During infantile chatter
Terrified students attempted to respond.
I called for silence, sudden silence, *excessive silence*. I told them
Jonathan Swift was a window-cleaner.

ANSWERS TO ODD-NUMBERED PROBLEMS

There was only you and me, like muons and pions in 1933,
as if the universe were composed like music.
We were in error, an error, a year out always.
The picture changed, like the canons,
and now we are just watching the tracks!

In a crowd like iron filings,
in a neighborhood of two bleak magnets,
I see your lack of an answer like a region.
But no answer was ever required
in this shower of soft iron filings, these busses and battleships.
—You loved the questions.

If the balloon rises above the ship,
what happens to the subject in the fire?
What about the diver in the diving bell,
how high could the water rise, as if it had no bottom?
Must we murder the inescapable creatures, those too slow or
    staggered by sand?

Three times I saw you like a surface
and floated on it completely submerged
and came back like a small piston to haunt you
on edge and placed in a dish like memory.
You are looking at your pregnant self a lot.

Then you attach me to a stone like a stone
and push me down like an empty glass
filled to the brim with a light like blood pressure.
All right. It's snowing on the tendrils.
It's snowing on the joke.
Your eye could not be more sensitive

to this luminous flux of dark units.
Efficient as a candle, you stood in those early days
as if your body was the source, and it was, like a streetlight on
   a desk.
You were absorbed in your passage through
this unreasonable mirror. Then scattered by the surface.

When I look away from you, the room is suddenly
   extinguished.

TO OUR CRITICS

I dreamed the dean of architecture taught me how to pitch
With a specific curve
I claimed I knew how to pitch that ball the softball the hard
But he had a specific curve in mind
I forgot my poetry all of it in notebooks like the sketch of a
    glove
Like lost leather gloves without irony to this day
You built a chair for everything
I dreamed I had forgotten proper names and proper nouns
Forgotten parts of bodies like a word
On an obscene blackboard in another dream
I dreamed the critics who deposed the dream had died
Of a brutal phantasmagoria in proscription
They had proscribed themselves

CROOKED LIGHTNING

Lightning is crooked because it takes
the path of lowest electrical resistance.
   —New York Times, *July 29,*
   1980

It hits the hill.
It is black lightning.
It tries the geometric tower and rebounds.
It detests it, the shifty shifter.
Rain fills our shoes with green pigment.
It spills the wave on the hill.
It costs a lot to soundproof against thunder.
As against a drill
That digs a hole for warm copper.
Plunging the unreal into the real or "vice versa."
The lightning takes steps.
Like the voice of one in the public library,
"When the lightning is black,
Happy is he who does not think life is too long."
Life is short and the lightning takes four short steps.
The first step is beyond the eye.
The second step reduplicates the picture like a doubt.
The third step erases hill and wave.
The fourth step illuminates what might have been a private
   embrace.

MAN ON A STONE SLAB

Voice never parts from body.

The stone could be your carpet,
Self-flier, but it's a shadowy block.
Cock on a block would be too chic
For this ancient precision?
He and his legs are mountains
Mountains of a pathos without strength.

"They" have almost eclipsed me
Eclipsed my left hand
That could be playing the caprices, say.

It's not an erection beneath this cloth
Just an early body boldly crosshatched
On the page with gravity and curls.
The nontubercular vision without a cry.
Young mouth still interests anyone.

The philosopher has his shadow,
The slab has none.
It is a bed for bad backs, good dust.
The funeral shadow at last escapes its drab.
It is a work-desk, for one paralyzed thing.

This is how one doubts pen and
Brown ink, tracing the traces, doubting
The doubts in the omphalos museum.
Folding the folds: It's the logic of lying down
Or logic lies down
But one is truly pinned there by the slab.

And do not call it a boat.
Effacing black chalk faces.

The adventure of the universe is a page
And reaps such imperfections
As are possible. Language, not a pencil.
Voice never parts from your body.
Hail, curator of the skin.

WORK IN SADNESS

If you are not permitted to strike
If you are not even permitted for example a mental strike
And you are going to be tortured for a slowdown
Then the next thing you can do is work in sadness
They say that is what Brazil is
Or for instance poor bread poor art
No that was getting something done quickly
The light is shining through the blinds so close it
The late May is really Hitlerian
I have lost my life through a delicacy
A real person would gun you down on the street
Or forget you or forget to gun you down on the street
Or forget the street or forget the word necklace

If the lying Cretans speak the truth

ANOTHER MARSCHALLIN

Time in the ground,
time like a gun and time like paper
time like a thing in a sandbar
let it die like a system,
it could happen like a sand-crab in the sand
or like sea-glass caught in a sandbar
like no one spurting out of nothing
You will see where the hero is, over
    a hidden stain
It is the anniversary of what
unlearning by rote like snowflakes
flying out of sleep to lie famously
About the famous twittering machine
    of you and me
like a lost cause in an alarm clock
and unlucky as the undertow there
Oh you have let yourself ebb
in the big march
But I bit into time as it fled
a ceaseless bite
I bit into it in the middle of the night
And I stood up alone like a girl in the street
alone in father's shop, where I
    mistook time for a hat.

A STUDY OF TWO LATE JULY FOURTHS

Now this little boat in hypnosis sets forth
It was a collaboration with cardboard bellman and beaver
    overboard
Giving up the agony of America or concrete rot
Like a realist forced to fix the swiftly falling buildings

This is how one departs from the forest of a drawing
Or tracing
My father the soldier stands upon the rock
Like the *Magnificat* sadly inverted and clinging to the riddle's
    neck

I am playing in my mother's lap
As she reads a book I will never see
My father put money on a house; it collapsed structurally
Give up give up the pavilion of the sun give up

Give up capital gain like capital losses
Capitulate taking it off like a cardigan
As one who hides a Broken Dutchman
In secret disseizin unlimited misgovernment give up the green
    helicopter under green trees

And all this Scotch tape turning color in the blue sun *gibs auf*
Alone and relative like bread and wine
As one descends the escalator to the gods desire and
    representation
And rage: at a humiliating height observe the death of the
    garden

Popeye averted in yellow skiff red bottom green spinach
And pink muscle raised like a toy Liberty
Memory bank, memory drum, memory track, memory switch
And the nymph says No, like sand sinking into oil at sea

Something big is happening to us
And it is driving me to the bottom
I know what washes away and who I am
Love, I am reading your lips

I the poor predictor predicted this catastrophe
Oxymoronic and disheveled the universe in summer pleasure
The eyeglasses look at you like a compact Spanish dictionary
The robot edges toward the conservator

You will sleep on this typewriter like a model prison
Reiterate that we did not kill you
As one who wants to be alone with his laughter
The raped Sabines come back and the rejected parts break
    through

At the edge of a gem
I met you as the object slipped into its own slipstream
Dancers swayed upon the helicopter
Over a broken bridge

THE SPHINX, AGAIN

To keep photographing the same ice
In the same river flowing beneath the same bridge
Trying to link the shadow of a word to another word
Staring into the same signs of signs for nothing

In a room like a model of a room after all
Near stairs which lead nowhere
Toward a bed split in two like a parody
Of the ground unsteady as a cage in space

The clock deleted the right time
As I have tried to delete you
Paint it on a fan; smear it on debris
Pan around the bodies draped in battered paper

Perhaps a trance will set you sane or poetry for nothing
You have lost the advantage of madness
You were grafted in the pain of a secret
To your own recessive until you reached tangency

WRITE OUT

I wanted to paint the night sky
So I considered a black Xerox
and my medium was correction pen fluid
the blue correction formerly too dry to work

I wetted the write out correction pen
and produced too many stars
by stamping down upon it
There are not too many stars in the night sky

I usually ruin such work
I have often been too symmetrical or busy
Often balanced these things out of fear
prudently distributing representations of miserable order

Not the dissertation on tohu bohu
I dreamed of as when the Zoroastrians considered
even the wandering planets
and followed them to the Hayden Planetarium of nights

Then I blotted the night sky onto sphinx skin
and disseminated baby blue stars
insipid stars now become Leigh Hunt's prison wallpaper
underneath which the cloying enjambments flow

Now I no longer see the crescent moon
I know it to be full
Would that I could take the part for the part again
Correction: The product is *white out* not *write out*

TO A SWAN

Then you were born, bit by bit, seeing silent and exciting.

You wanted to etch mental pain in the dust.
Then you were born out of buildings and pleasures and
    windows
and the cold painful and colored and fastidious
as a pill in a river: words bitterly little and alive.
Then you were born, swallowing dismissing and rising
Then you were born, angry and artful as a blue white swan.
Then you were born, painting loud appearances.
Then you were born, in the right place like a thumb and a
    tongue.
Then you were born, the animal in detail, impure and good.
Then you were born, breaking up rain ice and information.
Then you were born, fanatic nut to crack a riddle.
Then you were born, nude new and dissimilar.
Then you were born, in a lake like hidden art.
Then you were born, like a baked sculpture.
Then you were born, silent repetitive and good.
Then you were born, swallowing blue-gray and nude.
Then you were born, blind as usual and tempting like a
    tongue.
Then you were born, out of fanatic architecture and repeating
    windows
like art in a lake, like a pill in the rain, as
an angry swan in the cold dust swallows and rises in the cold
    wind.

UNTITLED

Lord
I have fallen in love with the harp again

vaguely, I saw
that the waves were turning black

it was a friendly ferry

that night you were born

ORDINARY UNHAPPINESS

TO A MUSE

Give me a first line, you who are far away.
The second line will almost write itself.
In times of pain, I open the dictionary.

Like a girl in the last row who will not say
The theoretical part of the dream was herself,
Give me a first lie, you who are far away.

A student laughs: I died once. Red is gray.
Cheat me like a quote, deceiving Elf.
In times of pain, I open the dictionary.

You who tried to carve this family in clay
Skeptical and frivolous as a filthy shelf
Give me another line, you who are far away.

It's a small freedom on a revisionary day
As a jay imitates the human on an elm—
In times of pain, I open the dictionary.

And in ordinary happiness, I open the dictionary.
The words remain, but the guards are gone for help.
Give me a last line, you who are far away.
In times of pain, I open the dictionary.

ORDINARY UNHAPPINESS

Ordinary unhappiness is a long poem.
Long enough. Irregular sonnet. Ordinary happiness: I nailed
    it to the field.
Ordinary, but what was ever ordinary about that wild shining
Object that you hung up like a coat hanger?

Now I see the women in bathing suits wrestling beside a
    margin
Of cool water and they have come to triple somersault
Out of the picture's edge. They want something beside
Unruffled surfaces hiding an enraged helpless *puer aeternus*?

The voice is a wandering part of the body.
I loved you, your lips that destroyed my posture, the snow
That masked the floor. Now I renounce the hysterical floor.

Like paradise or anti-bower or limitless elixir (alleged).
Last shadow of all to be strong as a shadow
Or dance our shadowy weakness as one possible dance dying
    in bed, fortunately.

ALL NIGHT SHOWS ARE CALLED
TRANSFIGURED NIGHT

I dreamt that poetry and medievalism
had a "joke contest" in which each
told jokes immediately after the other one
until one could not make up or remember a joke
and then lost his job
and they joked far into the night

Poetry was young and the joke
"Though she wears bracelets, Madame is unhealthy"
was a variant of the Islamic jokes medievalism was telling
and he thus had an easier time
imitating and subtly changing jokes medievalism had to invent
or "true ones"
such as Three boxes, one filled with
shapes, one with dots, one with interlocking cubes
and Barney Newman wiped the second one out saying
"I had to think fast, so I wiped out Impressionism"

MR AVERAGE VIEWER

Jerry Lewis once visited my home
Or actually I walked in and found him smoking with a friend
I loved your program Jerry Visits Jerry last night I said
Particularly when you said what you said against the war

Contra deum, Jerry, I cried
My wife didn't but it takes quarts of milk to wet some
(We both come from Newark) I asked him, "Is it true
What they said in Weequahic High about your tormenting
    teachers?"

You mean, he said, the *Cruel Jer*? Yes, I would stand on chairs
And torment them. I told them I did it too, worked with
    children now
Just like Jerry Lewis and his Marathons. You see
I watched those too, I said. You'd like children's works

I recited him one but he didn't seem too pleased.
Suddenly I wondered why I had been selected for this visit
His pal said, You have been picked as Mr Average Viewer.
Now a whole studio crew lounged by, and I prayed
      for you to come home.

DOUBTING THE DOUBTS

A map dropped from my hands
And a voice cried, From now on
You will proceed in darkness.
Alas, he laughed, that is true.

Was it a black map?
I do not remember.

We all love clarity.
But you love darkness.
But darkness is clear.

We do not know now and we will never know.
White night, perilous night.

ANOTHER VERSION OF THIN SNOW

The map drops from your hands
Like a voice. Or a map falls and a voice sounds,
From now on you will proceed in darkness. Alas, it's true. A
    map
Of one world on which I was permitted to paint one name.
One name, one island. On another hand,
"Sentimentality is far worse than death."
I don't know. What does *lepsy* come from?
Come from? To be taken; sleep; nymphs;
Or just to be had. As if we had been sleeping
Near that book by Malcolm, where all we know is that we
    wake
To find that arid map of Popeye on the pink bottomless
    barge:
"We do not know and we will never know" in tiny ink.
Though I know where you are going, influenced by a distant
    star
Glued like a grade to the back of a classroom wall.

REALISM

If the question you love is
    Rabbit or duck
Remember to dry the eye in the
    center of that creature
So that it gazes both over its beak
    and button nose
And looks to each side, at the profile
    of a young woman with feather and boa.

But now the woman is a purple crone.
It is a rabbit and/or duck or nothing
    but a sculpture
Bronzed in the sun of its broken neck:
    a base.
One says it would look more duckling on a
    pond, more rabbit in a warren,

But you were painting time again
And doubles and displaced the afterimage
    like a paint-can on a cloud.
You asked me what "totally white" could mean
And now we know: a lot of charcoal smeared
    upon those clouds, however.

All this for one who needs music
An ear for the divertimento of a nearly
    destroyed angel or opaque delinquent.
Too fastidious? The rabbit-duck grows up to be
    the size of a light-bulb.
You lie on your side, or it does, on a bed or
    a tomb or a thing.

THE ERRATICS

The star tries to rise but is forced down to the planetarium
Are we like swine following one another on bright yellow
    color aid paper
Or radiant white typewriter paper the wind blows on
With the fresh coolness of eraser fluid
Now we reach the fresh coolness of your breasts
Pretty boats are slicing the delicious waves
It is pleasure to board the barge you sit in like a burnished
    throne
Your feet are sprinkled with chilly foam
Sadly we argue like saddled horses
I see you in the distance as shiny as soda, as shiny as wine

A FAIRY TALE

Fairy tales were written in 1580
By 1600 sailing ships had improved

People in fairy tales run away
By 1600 they could run away further

Because the ships had improved

Faster than taxis
Further than India and you and Vasco da Gama

The whiteness of the whale
was written by a wretch

I lost my book of fairy tales
down by the magazine store

It was replaced by a taxi
Israel has no king

But if it has it should be you
Sweet singer of Israel

But it could not be
There is only one fairy tale

There are three persons in bed
I am sick and you inject me

With blood running through Rubens' veins
I will carry your luggage for you

The planes are not deterred by fog
By the little cloud of two hundred yards

A BOOK OF DOORS

1

The door is just a semidetached petal or
A small importance given to a face
Like carving in tracery or tracery in foliage
In the deep hollow of the unprinted page
And you come up with Donald Duck in the Greek doorway
Of Beauvais and nephews as a red rosette
There is no pain, but there is Uncle Scrooge sending us off
To bed like the simplest doors
In the slab, in the flap and leaf, the words fall
Paradoxically and why should I not transgress or close
As you see enclosed in the allied forest
Your own lips intensely dry and on your face no fear
Since the earliest door was Egypt—
Your face a single piece of wood
As a document of a dour integrity or the most of audacity
Hanging in the middle, still as a style

2

Though the door slopes inwards so that the width
Of it is Agamemnon's knees down to our time
You are no tiger but a door less boldly cut
Into a separate place like categories of this late date
Detached too as a door and remembering
There is no pain, but elaborately painful spirals
    are inlaid with pain
Door somewhat like a valve corresponding to the climate
    of your lips
In this country it was not necessary to frame them
But the paintings will show nothing if not love,
    pointing but only pointing

All ancient doors are here but Dido
Silent at the top and bottom of the night in
    basalt and granite intruding in Hell
But the history of permission had not been written yet
The hinge is not quite known but the change is known
All you deserve is my forgiveness, of course

3

Where doors are scarce, doorways continue
There is one amorphous door elastic and jelly-like
You are enclosed in the door as in the forest of the word
Or a boat riding the currents of ice over time
Like the notes in Poulenc playing Poulenc
As the narcissus said the jonquil itself a narcissus
I live alone in the fields of wandering electrons
And brushing past the past with something like hate
The doors dolorous as the doctors dating them
Where doors are scarce, one never enters
As a chord clustered to return through celebrated fog
The door a diamond externally but taken internally
    almost a wall
Where there is no door, notched men seeking the edges
For our part to slide through as it will be present again
    our breasts stained by paper

POEM FOR JOHN DEAN

At night I drive to the White House
    Hearing the laughter of Haldeman and Ehrlichman
I rush up to the auction block to say
    But you can't sell—sell my wife!

They pronounce their sibilants correctly
    Lips of long stapled cotton, stapled into narrow bands
As I tune into a broadcast of seeds dropping
    They pound the table for drowned briefcases

And I give it them as you undress
    With oil and grease
Making them drunk on licorice and pendants
    And they tip converting into cash

After pleasantries I speak falteringly
    Giving them the sound of *th th*
They detect my defects all of them
    Listening to the sound of your double scarves falling in

And I am unusually drunk and you unusually sweet
    Your mouth opens but they are gullets now
And the President comes out of his office and says
    "I have a desire for food

"I cannot bear your overt resentments
    "Please roll back your stockings of distinctive color
"I was a student of Zeno once on his painted Porch
    "How thick the rain is and gluey

It falls stuffing the President full of food
    And Zeno claps me with good wishes for the New Year
But they are handcuffs and I have too many hands
    Opening and closing like Icarus in a sea of wax

And I see also the Pythia floating on the bosom of Thetis
    Like pus in urine now
And a little brittle glazed and salty cloud shouts by
    I do not want to be your scapegoat anymore

And I stood farther back demanding the event
    After it had happened
While three female dancers yoked together like three celestial
    Bodies—the sun, moon, and earth—during eclipse

GROWING THINGS IN THE SICKROOM

Then set your imagination to work and plan a blank book
With porches and falls and kitchens and blank beds
It's lots of fun and makes the blank time pass like pastels
Quickly and primarily for those who are dry and good

Fastened to the floor to use our erased money
The black book was very easy and the results very smooth
Like a long piece of raffish joy passed through a needle
Now like a coarse needle now like a blunt bodkin our own
     variety of colored quietus

After a little practice the blank book is soft enough
To puncture and the patient sticks his head into the lion's
     "snout"
Your eyes are bodies and walls to enclose animals
But the blank book can be a wall also and a really effective
     doll

The blank book is not a bit of flesh-colored silk
And now comes the time to draw a watch face like
     a sister supplying the minutes
And the blank grows and outgrows the tumbler, transplanting
     it
This may be done without removing the blankness from the
     book

NUDE

Angry, hungry, and some other word—
There's only one other. False equivalents.
Always already monochrome is and was polychrome.
You were painting garbage, and I was
Every place at once, or many places at once,
Like a comb in your hair.
Pre-chamber, chamber;
Almond, bitter-almond.

A LOST POEM BY WHITEHEAD

When Alfred North Whitehead taught poetry at Princeton
He said the critic must not be color-blind, and F. Scott
    Fitzgerald
Heckled him in the back row, crying: All I want from many
    worlds
Is the fantasy of being a fiction. Whitehead wrote it out on the
    blackboard:

"The red world seems gray but it never ends, anti-heroic
"The green world freezes but is a map of other worlds,
    nested, replete
"The purple world connects to all others like a microchip's
    music from a lost key
"And the orange world is not ours to be completed, not ours
    to be abandoned.
    The orange world is also in the orange."

ANOTHER SONG
OR PURGATORY PURVEYOR

"If I can't have you"

I don't want a district
I don't want a district attorney
like Job
I don't want to get along get away
get beyond get together
geyser and geyserite
If I can't have you
get obtain procure
secure acquire gain win
earn
to come into possession
get is a very general term
obtain suggests expenditure
procure implies effort
win adds to gain
earn implies a correspondence
If I can't have you
steep tense and stark
If I can't have you
I don't want a garden outside Jerusalem
inanimate subject matter in a stream
so gentle the birth of death is not visible
Natural stigmata
a bundle of light rays
intersecting me at a single point
If I don't have you
a spring throws forth
intermittent jets of heated water
in whitish or grayish discretionary masses

You are an opal
If I can't have you
an intermittent fever
If I can't have you
dead or alive all or none
the darkroom preserved in solitude
where profane utensils
If I can't have you
a contest or struggle
in which now one side now the
other has the lead
If I can't have you
your large showy head of blue flowers
If I can't have you
spirit desire resentment
belly abdomen inclinations
"If I can't have you
I don't want nobody baby"

DECEMBER

Your nearness approaches like needle-shaped guns
desire an insufficient compass
in mind in nebulae and mist we meet obscurely in a bottle
Absent, distant, and ridiculous I go your way

PERSONAL AFFECTIONS

The smudge loves the smear
The brain loves a brainstorm
The nude loves the nozzle as tabula rasa loves a tablecloth
Venus loves Venetian blinds

The brain loves a brainstorm
The mezzotint loves the aquatint
Venus loves Venetian blinds
The sea serpents live by the seascape mixing time in music
   abed

The mezzotint loves the aquatint
You love the word "you"
The sea serpents live by the seascape mixing time in music
   abed
The prisoner loves the keeper

You love the word "you"
The keen-eyed fly loves the forbidden kaleidoscope
The prisoner loves the keeper
The smudge loves the smear

TRIP TO CYTHERA FROM CYTHERA

What is this island like a Venetian blind? it's Cythera
famous for clichés
looking and looking after all it's poor art's poor earth
Secret is a good word and so are parties for archaic Venus

Belly like an island venereal as a nation
in a jar full of roses
and where Baudelaire had an interview with a very singular
    object
it wasn't a temple it was a shadow

where the young priestess
in her robe full of broken passageways

His eyes were holes and
his intestines ran out like piss on a thigh, what a delicacy
    and their beaks had completely ripped out the penis

Oh you who live in Cythera, under a "suave sky"
Ridiculous hanged man, your problems are mine
Oh God I had
buried my mind in an allegory

On your island Venus where I found
my image hanging

LANDSCAPE WITHOUT YOU

after Friedlaender

You may be whiter than Galatea
More flowery than the street
more slender than ice and far sweeter
All the same I have taken up my pipe
    with a hundred reeds
The phonological element dominates in this
    cliff-enclosed gymnasium
Of a high-rise mountain heard by all
who are diminutive in my diminuendo
    Palely Polyphemus sings with his flute away from you
You were hardly hiding in the foreground as
    you listened to my song and combed or wrung out those
    notes
Like birds making contact from a distance
    You partly draped in a sheet of white paper
Lovers coding themselves on the blackest windows
Though I didn't always differentiate
    The birth of Bacchus and the death of Narcissus
your flesh from the flesh of other figures
Nothing moves but Polyphemus' music
I did not choose the moment when
Poussin did not choose   .
I did not choose the moment of the rock
The two lovers hurtling down like rocks
Smashed under the weight of this cruel drawing
Nor is my intention sunlight and viney happiness

77

OUTSIDE MOTHER'S ROOM

He knelt in the hallway, like a king
whose mistakes are cardboard.

A FRAGILE ART

At night, the contractors come
And as they come, they build the bedroom
Three bedrooms in your bedroom
Nearly finished but no room
Tables electricities half-beds like benches
No privacy for the married man
A mini-condo inside the co-op
Pregnancy and eviction
Eviction the opposite of architecture
And architecture the fragile art
Do not look for Blaise Pascal
There was no such man
He was a composite a folktale without
    history breaking all zones

A PRAYER

You have grown up the liveliest ghost
After all, you are not following chamber music
        Friday nights
in or reading newsy novels from the library
You have become a voice, more read now than reading

As one avoids your name but starts out
        singing it in travel
Our father, emphasis on our elder betters
With the pronouns not possessed but stolen like
        a royal teacup
Thy will be done, since we have little faith that
        ours ever could

On earth and heaven: two truncated rhomboids
Give us this day, give us one day, give it
Like water, and also give us water
Snow, music, and house I now avoid, as one avoids
        certain words, and they are words.

HOUSE (II)

What about an open mouth
Prince Myshkin was trying to cross the street
without hurting anybody
It's hard to make out Myshkin on the phonograph
Music for the idiots
Hedda Gabler tried to shoot me also
No, no don't!
And don't keep me writing the dissertations
on stage directions
In obeisance to the bloated judge
Who will more or less tawdrily judge us
On some respective Judgement Day
Somewhat more softly sweep the string
A jocular if Goethean task
The window is profoundly closed like the death mask
The eyes closed always on the word
Pink is distributed through the universe
And then the owner relents: a covenant
The universe is "let go"
Clouds are shunted quickly as through surgery
Stars, vacuous events, elevators in the air, last notes
One strand of hair was music
And later it doesn't fall like a finger
What's all this talk about snow for
Apollo sits on the house with Cassandra thinking
We could not all be Scotch-taped together
Though we tried, language knows we tried
The piano knows we tried
The linden tree knows as much
And any other so-called natural instruments
Paolo's Francesca smiled her famous smile
Which I kissed all smiling, waiting
Dictating, entranced

HOUSE (III)

I am not now nor have I ever been asleep
Turning towards the portable harpsichord
Underneath the garden where a snake was sensibly shot
All of the curses were equally impressive
All of the caresses
You nodded to me on the top of a wave
And beseeched me from the undertow
Broken chords up and down the beach
Yet one more repetitious narrative
And you swam out like a honeysuckle, like
  a revised toy airplane
The child inhabits
Vacillating near the sun's waxy odors
There is no advance in the arpeggio
Very quietly now the eyes go out of business
Dido refuses to write
Everyone is growing stronger from the load of
  empty pictures

HOUSE (IV)

Put the music back to the beginning;
Write that down, the impossible.
If the music turns off you'll have to
    reinstate it.
The island of Delos without the profane dead
All stairs—an island we must spell for you
A narrow moment narrowly cemented
Idle talk—revolted by the quadrivium
    that could be cut in glass
Dictating to blind daughters or typewriters
Comical precursors, music to be forgotten
To play backwards on broken ice, in different tempi.

That is not it—
By now we have come upon our theme of
    themelessness proper
As if meeting death halfway by a dart.
Where it most breathes I have observed
The is delicate
In search of a lost paragraph, lost lint,
    the fresh word or space
But what was so famous about freshness
What was so glamorous about it as glue
Gigantic horses upon the stolen pediment
Icarus didn't fear loss of control
So much as a certain grandiosity, a certain
    "what do I know"

But this could be much longer or
    tentative or substantial as syntax
Ever not quite master of those who do not know
The snow fell like spigots

Or was it from here
You might have mutilated the questions
From the point of view of every right dissolution
What the day knew or straight back to the
    cat's brain
Laughing beside homemade pillows
Homemade theodicy
But what one doesn't know are the geometries
    that might have described or created
    that possible world.

WHICH WORD

Long live the snowflake!
a savage and paradoxical remark,
not as savage and paradoxical as
long live death and yet—

Rain is on the window,
almost in the window:
Like the snowy parodies
We are all abused copies, in a sense.

The problem with the open plan
is it circumscribed a banjo
But why so angry? You were unique snowflake
Copies of a copy!

Que sais-je? Good title for a press:
prison-house press.
I didn't think I could, I am without you
without addressee, slipped away, the code, content,
tongue trod upon, obstacles overcome

Blindness and blindness and Narcissus
reclines bluely beside the lake
which steadily does not reflect him
And Echo was bones.

No no no no a good beginning
to a radiating strawbridge connecting
novelties perfumes displays
to perfume novelty displays
And speechlessness unpainted or gray.

But the daisies and the hawkweed
still drip from the painting.
It was so wet the dust loved it.
Surrounded by pastoral in the cardboard house.

THE BOY WHO LOVED BUBBLES

Because a universe is one bubble
of black bubbles, and yet
a boy is watching always with bloody eyes
—a boy who loves bubbles—
as a black stone rises beside our sleeping head

Tame at the end of a stem
it may not burst like paper
into fifty sheets
as he knows who stripes his notebook with lithographs
Inserting his pen into his mother's black purse
he covers it he discovers it in a glance
with schedules and weeks and a bitten newspaper
But he is looking for writing, the black bubbles

Now what emerges is the antonym
a clipping as colorful and useless as a singularity
and mother's black planet
Now bubble and syllable break in the evening air

You were not really listening to the last sentence
Because you could not see it, the transparent dump we live in
     like a frothy star
Now you are really listening so I will tell you the end

Inside the bubble is another bubble, of course
Inside the stone is a star of pain

Exploding like an accident, the wild syllable, wet
The king delighted by forbidden hair
Poems of birth that were not poems of birth
Music and panic engendered by a prophet without vision
The nostril of an injured monster flaring with a pill

Toby and Nairobi, Thetis the magician
Stigmata on the wand Difficulties of the stateless A cab ride
    wrong
    A ride home Relays
Reading in the dark nothing but the kaleidoscope of the last
    century

David Shapiro, recipient of the American Academy and Institute of Arts and Letters' 1977 Morton Dauwen Zabel Award in Poetry, was born in 1947 and was a professional violinist in his youth. he is the author of six volumes of poetry, including *January, Lateness,* and *To An Idea.* Since the publication of his first book in 1965, he has published poetry, art, and literary criticism in *The New Yorker, Partisan Review,* and *The Paris Review,* and he is widely anthologized and translated. He has received fellowships from both the National Endowment for the Arts and National Endowment for the Humanities, and is a member of the International Art Critics Association and PEN.

Shapiro has taught at Columbia University, Brooklyn College, Princeton University and Cooper Union. He is currently Associate Professor in Art History at The William Paterson College of New Jersey.